NORTH DEVON

PHOTOGRAPHS TO REMEMBER HER BY

INTRODUCTION

It all began in Berlin . . . a book about North Devon and it began in Berlin? Let me explain . . . my wife and I were visiting Berlin, and one evening in our hotel we struck up a conversation with an elderly American gentleman. It transpired that his great-grandfather, who incidentally fought with Wellington at Waterloo, hailed from Barnstaple, North Devon, before the family emigrated to the New World. Could we possibly send him a souvenir booklet showing scenes of North Devon, as he was interested in knowing what the area looked like? . . . easy . . . no problem, . . . be delighted. Visits to many bookshops in North Devon produced souvenirs of the 'West Country', 'Devon' (with hardly a mention of anywhere North of Exeter), or 'Exmoor' two thirds of which is Somerset. There were detailed guides to walks in North Devon, guides listing the accommodation available in North Devon, where to eat, where to go for entertainment, even detailed history books, but when it came to a photographic souvenir of North Devon . . . Nothing! "You're a photographer — produce your own!" . . . My wife's words kept coming back to me . . . why not? Surely there must be others who just wanted to remember what the area looked like?

The idea took root, and here it is . . . I hope you enjoy it, as I hope our elderly American Gentleman will . . . that reminds me, I must remember to post him a copy . . . now where did I put his address?

Text and photographs © Bernard Warner (L.R.P.S.) 1991
Published by Bernard Warner, 2 Whitemoor Cottages,
Loxhore, Barnstaple, North Devon, EX31 4SR

All rights reserved. No part of this publication may be reproduced, stored in a retrieval system, or transmitted in any form or by any means, electronic, mechanical, photocopying, recording or otherwise, without the prior permission of the publishers.

ISBN 0 9518486 0 7

Printed by Colorworks, Unit 22, Calow Lane Industrial Estate,
Hasland, Chesterfield, Derbyshire, S41 0DR, U.K.

Clovelly Village, from the Harbour

Looking down Clovelly

In Clovelly, deliveries are normally made by sledge

A side street in Clovelly

Looking East from Harbour Wall, Clovelly

Rooftop and Harbour, Clovelly

Fishermen at Clovelly

9 Boat trip from Clovelly (Lundy Island in Distance)

Coast near Clovelly, looking towards Westward Ho!

Bideford and River Torridge

Bideford bridge, showing the Lundy supply ship 'm.s. Oldenburg'

A view of Appledore from Instow

A view of Barnstaple from near Bradiford

The Long Bridge, Barnstaple. There has been a bridge here since the 14c.

Queen Anne's walk,
Statue of Queen Anne dated 1709.

Barnstaple Square. (With The Museum of North Devon in the background)

Pilton High Street. (One of the oldest areas of Barnstaple, dating back to the 9c)

Local farmers meet at the Cattle Market every Friday

Barnstaple Panier Market

Barnstaple Panier Market

'The Personal Touch', with photographs of all contributors. (Panier Market)

Forecourt to Barnstaple's modern Library

Gammon Walk Shopping Area

Near Old School House, Church Lane, Barnstaple

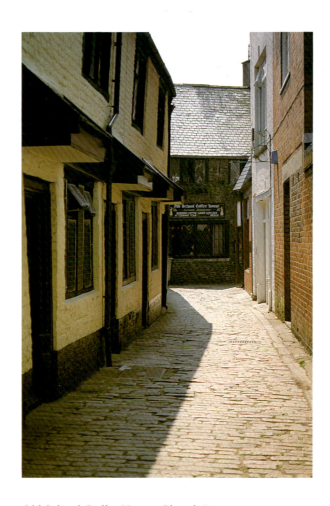

Old School Coffee House, Church Lane.
Site of the first Free School in Barnstaple. 1659

Penrose Alms Houses, Litchdon Street. Built 1627.

Courtyard, Penrose Alms Houses

Elderly Resident sat outside Penrose Alms Houses

27 Night View of Barnstaple

Thatched Cottage near Prixford

Muddiford

Leafy Lane near Muddiford

Saunton Sands, early morning

Croyde Bay

Croyde Village

A Meadow full of wild flowers near Croyde

Woolacombe Sands, looking towards Putsborough

Beach near Mortehoe

Arlington Court Gardens. (A National Trust Property)

Arlington Court, with Carriage and Horses in foreground (A N.T. Property)

The Local Telephone box at Arlington

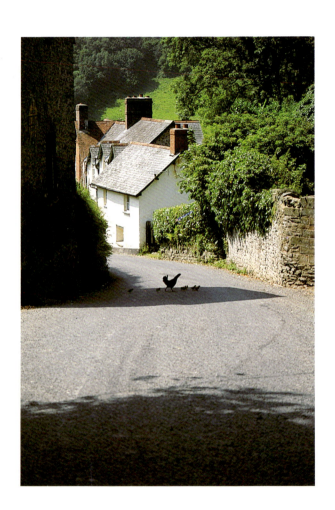

'Stop' children crossing, Loxhore Cott.

A view of Kentisbury Ford from Arlington

Horse Riding near Arlington

Wistlandpound Reservoir

Valley between Loxhore and Shirwell

The Torr's Coastline near Ilfracombe

Capstone Head, Ilfracombe

Hillsborough from Capstone Parade, Ilfracombe.

A view of Ilfracombe Harbour

The High Street, Ilfracombe

Market town of South Molton

On the outskirts of South Molton

Old Bridge at Challacombe

Berrynarbor Village

A view of Combe Martin

Combe Martin Beach with the tide out

Combe Martin from the beach

Pond on the outskirts of Combe Martin

Sunset near Arlington Beccott

Village of Parracombe

Cottages at Lynbridge, Near Lynton

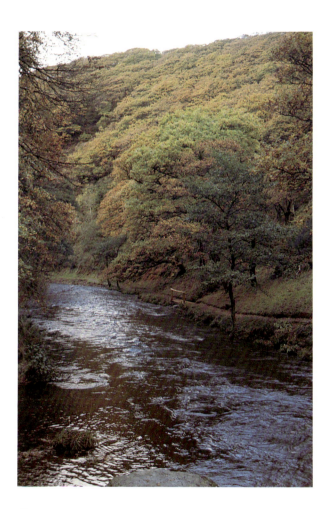

The East Lyn River near Watersmeet

Lynmouth Street

Exmoor, showing East Lyn Valley in the distance

Exmoor, near Brendon

Foreland Point, Countisbury

Sunset, near Arlington